live
BLUEGRASS

MUSIC

Compound Word

by Trisha Speed Shaskan   illustrated by Sara Gray

compound word two words put together to make one word with a new meaning

Editor: Christianne Jones
Designer: Hilary Wacholz
Page Production: Melissa Kes
Art Director: Nathan Gassman
The illustrations in this book were created with acrylics.

Picture Window Books
A Capstone Imprint
151 Good Counsel Drive
P.O. Box 669
Mankato, MN 56002-0669
877-845-8392
www.capstonepub.com

Printed in the United States of America in
North Mankato, Minnesota. 022010 005708R

All books published by Picture
Window Books are manufactured
with paper containing at least
10 percent post-consumer waste.

**Library of Congress Cataloging-in-
Publication Data**
Shaskan, Trisha Speed, 1973-
If you were a compound word / by Trisha Speed
Shaskan ; illustrated by Sara Gray.
p. cm. — (Word fun)
Includes index.
ISBN 978-1-4048-4771-2 (library binding)
ISBN 978-1-4048-4776-7 (paperback)
1. English language—Compound words—Juvenile
literature. I. Gray, Sara, ill. II. Title.
PE1175.S43 2008
428.1—dc22   2008006352

Looking for compound words?
Watch for the BIG words throughout the book.

Special thanks to our advisers for their expertise:
Rosemary G. Palmer, Ph.D., Department of Literacy
College of Education, Boise State University

Terry Flaherty, Ph.D., Professor of English
Minnesota State University, Mankato

If you were a compound word ...

MINNESOTA

Lake Superior

Wisconsin

Lake Michigan

Mississippi River

Iowa

Illinois

Missouri

Kentucky

Tennessee

Arkansas

Mississippi

Louisiana

GULF OF MEXICO

N
W · E
S

3

... you could be a SWASHBUCKLER or a SHIPMATE traveling on a **SOUTHBOUND STEAMBOAT** down the Mississippi River.

If you were a compound word, you would be two words put together to make one word with a new meaning.

6

At the **HEADWATERS** of the Mississippi River in Minnesota, a **DRAGONFLY** rests on a **SANDBAR**.

LAKE ITASCA

If you were a compound word, you could have fun in any season.

During the **SUMMERTIME** in Minnesota, a **BULLFROG** swishes through the **SEAWEED.**

During the **WINTERTIME** in Wisconsin, cows ice-skate across the frozen **WATERWAY** and play in SNOWDRIFTS.

If you were a compound word, you could be a form of transportation.

In Iowa, a bass family runs out of gas while relaxing on a **HOUSEBOAT.**

They don't call a
MOTORBOAT or a SAILBOAT.
They call a TOWBOAT.

TOWING

If you were a compound word, you could be a playful animal.

In Missouri, **WOODCHUCKS** leave their burrows to **SUNBATHE**.

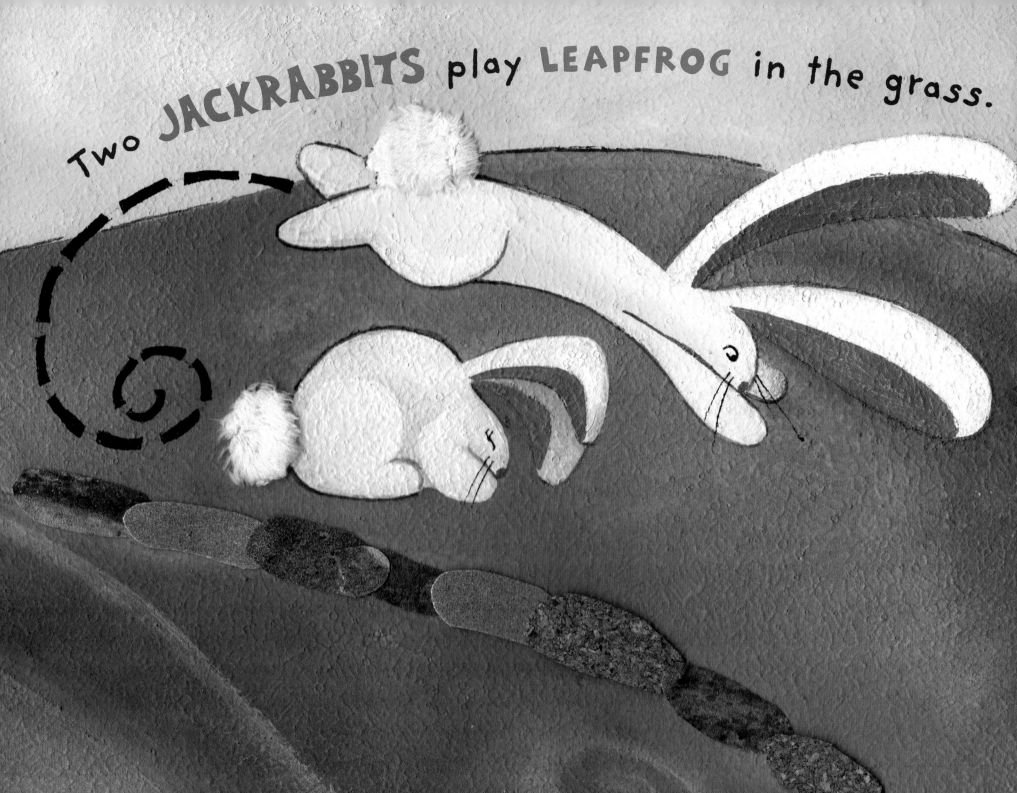

Two JACKRABBITS play LEAPFROG in the grass.

If you were a compound word, you could describe the weather.

In Illinois, **THUNDERCLAPS** boom!

A **RAINSTORM** floods the river and rocks the boats.

If you were a compound word, you could be an animal enjoying different kinds of music.

Live Bluegrass

LIVE MUSIC

In Kentucky, a **SOFTSHELL** turtle plays **BLUEGRASS.**

In Tennessee, wintering WATERFOWL swing to ROCKABILLY.

17

If you were a compound word, you could describe nature.

In Arkansas, SONGBIRDS play in the HARDWOOD forest. Then they rest in the GRASSLANDS.

18

In Mississippi, trumpet **HONEYSUCKLES** sound their horns. **MAYPOPS** spin like **PINWHEELS.**

If you were a compound word, you could be different types of food.

In Louisiana, an alligator eats **CRAWFISH** pie and HUSHPUPPIES.

20

You could put things together and dream about a **LIFETIME** of **CAREFREE** adventures ...

... if you were a compound word.

MAKING YOUR OWN COMPOUND WORDS

Here are two lists of words that can become compound words when joined together. Join each word from the left column with a word from the right column. For example, *night* plus *gown* becomes *nightgown*. Use a dictionary to check if the word you made is a compound word. After you have created the compound words, write a story using all of them!

wind	storm
night	fall
bull	pour
rain	gown
down	frog

Glossary

compound word—two words put together
    to make one word with a new meaning
definition—the meaning of a word
headwaters—the beginning of a stream
swashbuckler—an adventurer

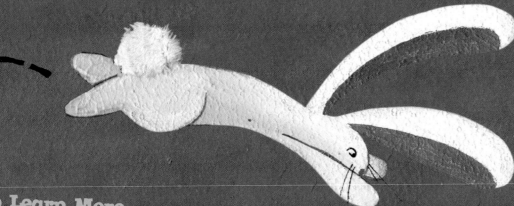

To Learn More

More Books to Read

Maestro, Betsy. *All Aboard Overnight.* New York: Clarion
    Books, 1992.
Rondeau, Amanda. *Base + Ball = Baseball.* Edina, Minn.:
    Abdo, 2004.
Walton, Rick. *Once There Was a Bull...frog.* Salt Lake City:
    Gibbs Smith Publishers, 1995.

On the Web

FactHound offers a safe, fun way to find Web sites
related to topics in this book. All of the sites on
FactHound have been researched by our staff.

1. Visit www.facthound.com
2. Type in this special code:
    1404847715
3. Click on the FETCH IT button.

Your trusty FactHound will fetch the best sites for you!

Look for all of the books in the Word Fun series: